AF417872

WORDS AND IMAGES

WORDS AND IMAGES

**A Poetry Collection
by Lenka Dvorcakova**

Copyright © 2023 by Lenka Dvorcakova
ISBN: 9789403719139
Cover design and illustrations: Lenka Dvorcakova

CONTENTS

PART I: AWAKENING

DARKNESS

I've fallen in love
with the darkness,
but I can hardly hear
what she wishes to tell me
through the silence.

I've been trying to read her lips
to solve it in Morse.
She says,
"It would be liberating
to finally see the source
of light,
but I can't commit suicide.

Raise the blinds and let me disappear
without any signs of fear
because I'll be back by night."

She means well,
but I know now:
Letting her go has somehow
been liberating for me, too.

Now we live in peace,
occasionally side by side
like old lovers,
both in need of light.

I WANT TO UNDERSTAND

Why
are wings called wings;
do goldfish grant only three wishes;
does light shine while darkness hides
under a coat of stars?

Why
can we see a variety of colors
only through rose-tinted glasses?
Why do I have to lose you
in the abyss
enveloped by skulls and bones?

Why
can't we control ourselves
with a remote,
but the television can control us?
Why don't humans know
the secret language
of animals?

I want to understand,
but sometimes it seems
like I'm the only one
who cares about these things.

So I close my eyes
and hear a voice gently say:
*Don't think too much,
dear child. Just play.*

MIRRORS

I'm running away
from strangers in a mirror maze,
but everywhere I turn,
I see darkness staring at my face.

Unfamiliar figures are chasing me,
so I'm speeding up, breaking the glass.
It's so freezing out here that my hands are shaking
and I can sense the moisture of expansive grass.

My breaths are fast and deep,
creating a dense haze.
I can't see that clearly.
How can I escape this maze?

Blurred reflections
of my identity
make me wonder
what kind of entity
I am.

I feel you deep within me,
so I saunter closer to the mirror,
but as soon as I face this fear,
it sinks in the depths of a clear river

There's no one to find;
The maze is not real.
It's all in my mind—
the mind that isn't healed.

IN SEARCH OF GOD

Being in search of God
is a roller-coaster journey:
Is he a man or is she a woman?
It was too early to ask.
But after some time passed
and I kept learning,
God took off the mask.

Gazing into familiar eyes
in the clear water's mirror,
I found something,
and it whispered:
Come nearer, come nearer.

"Let me be awake.
Do not sleep anymore.
Do not be afraid
to peer into the core
of your heart.

That's where I've always been.
Close your eyes, and you'll see what I mean.

Trust me.
I know who you truly are.
In that core, there's so much more
than an infinite star."

TRANSIENCE

"Nothing lasts forever,"
they say.
Life's a game; you should play.

Trauma and pain are waiting for you
to transform them.

Take a plane
to a destination called Paradise,
where everything's fine
and full of sunshine and butterflies,
a new state of mind.

I admit that the path is hard to find,
but it's worth it, my friend.
Otherwise, you will have to
play your part
in other people's games.

Find a flame
hidden deep in your heart.
Take a journey to real treasure,
where Ending's just a place
in which you can start
again.

So please, find that flame
and greet it with a smile
every single day
'till the rest of your life.

TIME

Time is ticking
for the millionth time.
Are you truly living
or is life passing you by?

Tick-tock
for the millionth time.
Please don't chase material things
and then call them *"mine"*
because they will never be.
Instead, open your heart
and set yourself free.

Blossoms on a tree,
then snowflakes falling down again.
Tick-tock.
Come on; take my hand,
and let's transcend to another plane.

But shall we do it now?
Later might be too late
if our souls will be taken
to the higher gate.

Tick-tock.
I hear it for the millionth time,
so I get up from bed
to see the sun shine.

And I feel so perfectly fine.

MASTER OF FREQUENCY

Masters of Frequency…
Shall you be one of them
with a heart full of faith
while creating your path?

It is unique because you're on a quest.
The power of a deed is written in the past.

Enter with a luminous lantern
into a dark cave full of those who truly need it
and show them how to heal themselves,
because in that, you'll find your meaning.

Follow your intuition
like a Sagittarius who aims for the unseen.
Grow, change, move forward!
Just don't get stuck in between.

Master of frequency,
full of joy and wisdom,
now is the time
to build the spiritual kingdom
you've always dreamed about.
So, believe in yourself;
It's the same as believing in God.

Take a deep breath in
and slowly rise above!
Change the world
in the name of unconditional love.

TRAVELER

I'm a traveler
wandering between lands
and dimensions,
admiring *a world in a grain of sand*
while breaking conventions.
I follow a whisper
that only I can hear
and step forward
without fear.

The beauty of nature is taking my breath.
God's perfect plan:
birth and death.
My quest lands in my imagination
as soon as a celestial voice whispers:
"This is the last station."
My heart almost jumps
out of my chest!
So this is what it feels like
to be blessed…

I've traveled too far.
I cannot go back in time;
I don't even want to
now that I've finally found the divine
in me.

I'm a traveler.
Just thought you should know
before your heart falls in love...

SECRET

I live in a cozy house
not far from yours.
It's full of sunlight
with opened windows and doors.

I'm a millionaire,
but nobody knows,
except the Source
'cause it loves me the most.

The house is surrounded by colorful trees
and an enchanting lake.
I'm there holding my own silver keys,
my heart full and my mind awake.

Ahead of time,
I'm starting from the end.
Is it a crime
that I read a sign it sent?

I often immerse myself in spiritual books,
for they are my private anchor.
Within them, every sign can be found;
Feeling is the answer.

Laws of the Universe
are challenging to explain.
To understand, you need to take
a deeper dive into your brain.

One, two, three…
I'm living my dreams,
in perfect order
with infinite schemes.

SYSTEM HACKER

A perfect system designed
to forget who we are…
It's a trap;
We are already in too deep
and have gone too far.

Endless rules and regulations
keep deceiving every nation.
We're dreaming about brand-new cars
and hotels with five stars.
We're chasing money in survival mode.
My friend, it's time to break the code!

Material things can fulfill us
but only for a while,
only to find we're empty again
and, in front of us, is another trial.

So when there is doubt,
just take a deep breath in
and leave behind your bones and skin.

Open your eyes to Eternity
and feel the love of Unity.
The Source will bring you light,
which will enlighten the night
and fearlessly shine from within
to help you become what you've always been.

With a heart all joyful and warm

that's ready to face the greatest storm,
you're a warrior traveling at the speed of light
to a yet-to-be-known, transcendental height.

Now the system has lost its power
and every second feels like an hour.
You've opened your heart and woken up the nations
from this long-lasting simulation.

RIDDLE

As time stopped,
I passed to the other side
and observed motionless figures
in the colors of traffic lights.

I meandered through the scene
'till I found myself in the middle.
With a halo around my head,
I was trying to solve a riddle.

Barefoot, treading on broken glass
that reflected the face of a burning sun,
I couldn't solve the riddle,
but the messengers kept saying that I was the one.

"With a simple thought, it starts
and with a matter, it ends"
was the sacred knowledge hidden
under the veil of hot sands.
The solution was obvious
for the one with an open mind.
Now I looked with a different eye.
How could I be so blind?

I realized I was the creator all along
with more power than I had ever thought.
I had finally found my peace
because the riddle was solved.

NEW ERA

You and me, we're the same,
made of atoms on this plane.
God's reflection is in our eyes,
a strange Big Bang where no one died.

Great things are coming;
A New Era has begun.
Don't fear the change;
It's all part of the plan.

You and me, we inspire,
with our hearts full of fire.
Keep the faith, and I'll return
after lessons I need to learn.

HOME

Indeterminate future…
Just around the corner, there's a street
with the same address of a place
where we were supposed to meet.

There's no end without a beginning
and no logic behind my feelings.
Endless rhythm: as above, so below—
Nothing rests in this infinite cosmic flow.

I'm leaving a message here
that may seem meaningless at first glance,
but if a poet writes it,
it makes complete sense.

The same address you gave me
a few million years ago
may be lost now,
but in the end, we'll be back home.

DESIRE

In my blood, I find a blazing fire.
I'm on this planet to spread desire.
Traveling up and down, carried by the waves,
I'm always excited to explore a new place.

The song of the siren plays in my heart.
You're falling for me right from the start.
My touch electrifies faster than light.
You're already burning; it's too late to fight.

The chemical reaction is instant,
the magnetism's strong.
Don't avert your gaze, darling.
Listen to my song.

You will be illuminated,
but what carries the higher power?
It's a gift. Trust me—
I've never been a liar.

I'm a lightbulb over your head,
electricity along a black wire,
an energy transfer that spreads
an everlasting desire.

CONTACT

I asked for contact
and said that I'm a fearless kind,
then sent a secret code
through my wireless mind.

I shared with them my loving thoughts
and intentions
with high frequencies and vibrations.

I'm still waiting for them to appear,
night by night and year by year.
When the sky turns pink
and I see the lightning,
I feel calm; it's not frightening.

Maybe I've already met them
many times before…
In human shapes and forms,
perhaps they've knocked at my door.

And I let them enter—
these beings of light,
straight into my heart center
in the middle of the night.

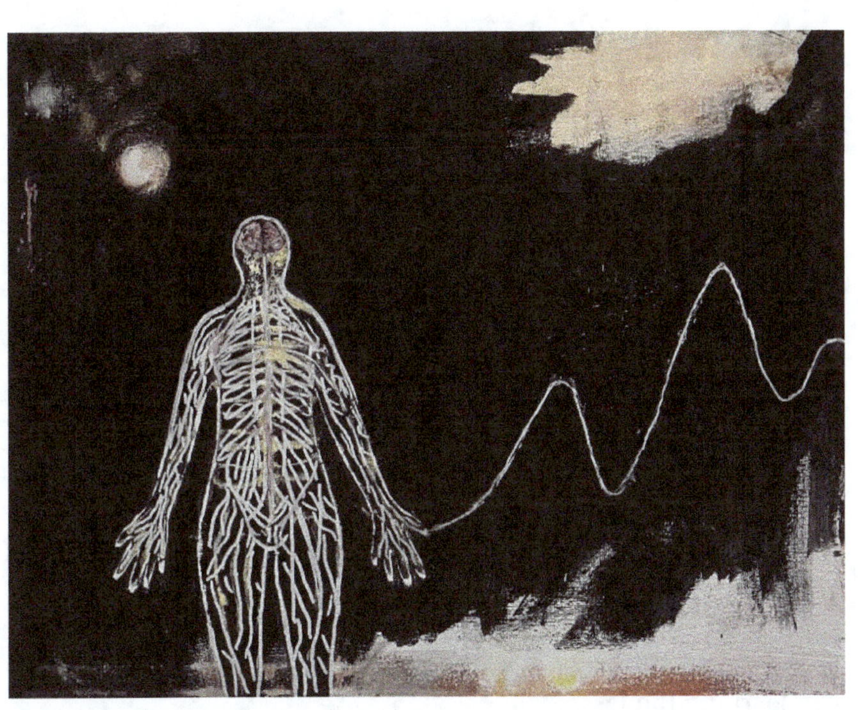

LESSONS

Different people with the same situations
are all teachers with changing faces
in a perfectly designed simulation
built upon a solid basis.

"I failed a challenging test!"
"Find the next one behind a corner."
I said I did my very best,
but they want me to pass it with honor.

I have been slapped at least a thousand times
before I started to read between the lines:
It's the same situation with a few small changes.
People I used to love are now just strangers.

I learn a new lesson every day:
Evolve or repeat... There's no other way.

"What is it trying to teach me?"
I always ask.
The most valuable knowledge
becomes an insurmountable task.

I'm learning the lessons;
It'll simply never end.
But I don't mind
if it gives me strength...

PROCESS

I see myself from a few years ago:
a person I no longer recognize.
Like an endless flower, I grow,
in the Fibonacci sequence to new heights.

Like a snake that sheds its skin,
I leave my past self behind.
I'm like a butterfly that had to go through darkness
to enjoy the most beautiful flight.

And just like a tree that moves through the seasons,
I had a crown that lost all its vivid leaves,
but after Winter, Spring arrived again,
making me bloom and freeing me from my grief.

Now, I have faith and follow my dreams,
for miracles come when someone believes.
The process is arduous, but it'll get better.
The Universe is joining it all together.

ENERGY

It's the energy; now I know.
We're running in a divine flow.
Our heavy feet are on a treadmill that never stops
and our faces are drowning in countless drops.

We're all part of the one;
Everything's connected here.
A Mother knows what's happening with her son;
She's miles away, but her feeling is real.

There's a constant transmutation
with genetic alteration.
The golden energy in our body can heal.
A tingling sensation is a sign that it's near.

It's something from a higher power,
something that we can't explain.
Try to meditate, and you'll feel that fire
that's pulsing through every vein.

We keep running, even when we're tired,
'cause our souls are raging,
and as we vibrate higher,
the whole world keeps changing

BLACK SHEEP

A black sheep is lost
in three-dimensional space,
where the majority is mundane,
but that's not true in her case.

The sheep has never belonged
to the same flock
and always goes so far away
for her leisurely walks.

At three o'clock in the morning,
the sheep is back with a warning:
You, black sheep, better behave
or you'll end up in your own grave!

But she ignores them all,
only interested in her goal.
So, she packs up her stuff and leaves the flock
before sunrise at three o'clock.

The goal of the sheep is to explore
and find something that is worth living for;
to create an eternal mark in this space
and overcome fear when it stares her in the face.

Many obstacles get in her way,
but she bravely continues to play.
Hunger, enemies, tricky situations?
In her inner voice, she has found her salvation.

Only few know where the sheep is now.
The rest keep asking: *What? Where? How?*
They still wander and they still talk
about her at three o'clock…

DIARY

I have a diary where I talk to God.
Some find it funny, others find it odd.
But I don't care what people think.
If they're judging, I let that ship sink.

I write down my thoughts and dreams
and wonder what it all means.
Then, I patiently wait every time
for a synchronicity or a sign.

Afterward, God talks to me
and leads me on the right path.
To understand these patterns,
I don't need physics or math.

It speaks in the language of love,
in a cosmic vibration.
It's at the center
of every creation.

It's golden energy in the pineal gland
like pyramids standing on hot sand.

I think again with no clue,
not quite sure what is true.
I'm searching endlessly into my mind
for the answers that I can't find.

So I ask the God again:
What is your perfect plan?

And It replies without hesitation:
To experience myself in perfect vibration.

GOLDEN AGE

We're heading to the Golden Age
ready to break out of our cage.
We've been trapped in melancholy for countless years,
trying to hold back all our tears.

We are prisoners of cruel materialism,
trying to reach peak idealism.
We listen to the government and politicians,
forgetting about our own inner visions.

But memories keep slowly coming back,
and they're getting us on the right track.
Money won't be able to control us anymore;
There's always something else that we're longing for.

In love and harmony, we will all live here,
in a Golden Age on this sphere.

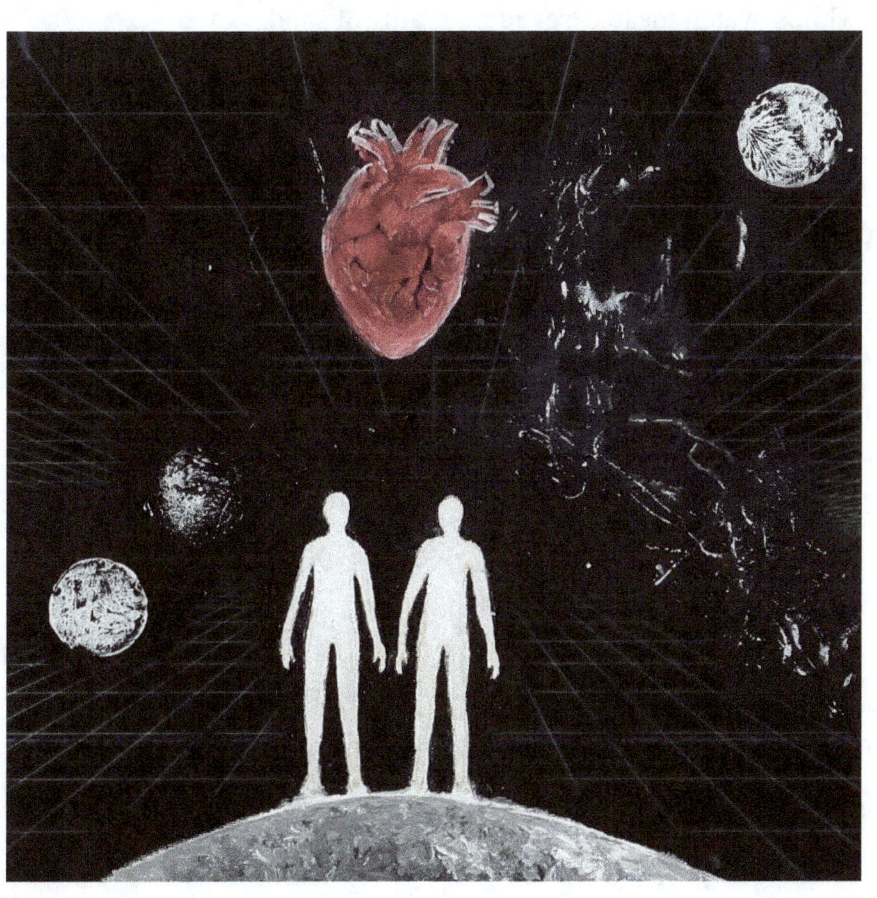

PROPHET

With dreams full of visions
and a forgotten paradise in my hands,
I'm trying to remember the past
while I watch these descending grains of sand.

I hold an antique hourglass
that counts every beat of my heart
as I travel through a black hole
and then back to the start.

I feel it coming:
transformation of consciousness.
The change is near—
a treasure locked behind an ancient door.
Soon, everything will be clear.

The truth has been spoken
quietly into my ears.
I've been searching for answers
for what seems like thousands of years.

A pupil became a prophet
and is the operating mind of this game,
like an astronaut flying through space
with a spirit that cannot be tamed.

BY THE SEA

Far away by the sea,
water is flowing
as I dream.
My eyes are closed,
but my mind's awake
full of familiar pictures
from different ages.

Years ago, a prophet said
that something will change
in my head.
Little screws and an iron shield
that protects thoughts
in an electric field.

Who am I? Do you know?
It seems like I forgot my role.
Little screws, a pulsing heart…
Nothing's better for my art.

Far away by the sea,
my eyes are closed
as I dream.

FOOL

As you head towards the unknown,
who knows what it'll bring.
Many people are afraid,
but a fool just prances and sings.

The fool is always ahead of you,
walking miles with long legs,
and knows the answers to questions
that others are too scared to ask.

Constantly ready for an adventure,
the fool is packed within a few minutes
and doesn't need that much
on a journey without limits.

We are like the restless fool
who's fighting for something of worth,
and we're on the edge
of this changing world.

PART II: LOVE POEMS

IN THE MOONLIGHT

In the moonlight, I see your body
lying next to mine.
I touch your soft skin
that smells better than flowers
in space and time.

I slowly pull you close to me;
this attraction, stronger than gravity.

The tips of my fingers
are playing with your expectations
and unconditional love
as we travel through dimensions.

You and I,
secret lovers in the quantum field
with infinite possibilities,
but we can't unite until we're healed.

In the moonlight, I see your soul
and the cosmic sign.
I hear your deep breaths
and your voice saying:
You're mine.

IT'S BEEN JUST A MOMENT

I swear, it's been just a moment…
It was only yesterday
when I held you in my arms,
smelled your hair
and neck,
knowing that nobody else
smells like you,
my love.

It's been just a moment,
and I want to say so much,
but every time I try,
only silence
comes out of my mouth.

It's been just a moment,
and now I'm here,
remembering your smile
that constantly turned my world
upside down.

You became the most beautiful
part of me,
continually running
through my mind.
Yes, it's true:
I've been thinking about you
with every single beat
of my heart.

I've always loved you.
What else can I say?
Now I'm opening my eyes
to just another day.

I swear that it's been just a moment…
It was only yesterday
when I held you in my arms,
smelled your hair
and kissed your lips.

…Or was it all just another dream of mine?

FATE

Loneliness
doesn't feel like it used to;
It's a new state of happiness
with colors of truth
in your eyes.

In this endless universe,
I try to count the stars,
but I'm losing myself
every time you smile.

I'm on my way to Mars
and holding you a place
a few million miles
through cosmic space.

A sudden flashback…
Your red lips say:
It can't be a sin if it feels like love.
Energy stronger than ever before
pulls me towards you.

I know I should say no,
but I feel like I could never fight
with this kind of love.

So I surrender and wait;
Divine timing won't be late.
I promise to see you again
if it's our fate…

ONCE UPON A TIME

Once upon a time,
I came to a different land,
only to find out that the beginning
is just another end.

I missed mountains
and the sun in the sky,
but I found one
deep in your eyes.

So light and high,
no time had ever felt better
as the one
that we spent together.

I didn't know
that the sun in the sky,
so bright and high,
could burn me alive.

Sweet resurrection,
action and reaction,
atoms form molecules—
you and I
in this game for fools.

I kept daydreaming
about every touch and feeling.
So close yet so far away,
love grew stronger

every day...

Once upon a time,
I heard angels singing
that the painful end
is just another beginning.

LOVE

My love is greater than the galaxy,
but if you're unable to see,
close your eyes and just try to feel.
Maybe I could help you heal
every wound and scar,
and show you the most magnificent star

under the magic of darkness.

Next to you…
There's nowhere I'd rather be—
so close, holding hands,
just you and me.

I wish I could kiss your lips
and say the words you long to hear,
but I know we live in different worlds,
my dear.

However,
the separation is external
and even though I miss you, I know
this is eternal
'cause I fell in love with your soul.

DRAGONFLIES

You gave me a gift that will last forever,
something intense right from heaven.

I see dragonflies;
In the same patterns, they fly.
And as I watch them,
I try not to cry.

I feel the love and the sadness;
I'm too deep in this madness.
Translucent wings reflect light
and bring memories into my mind:

> *With joy on your face*
> *that seemed out of control,*
> *you explained*
> *that many people love butterflies,*
> *but dragonflies have touched your soul.*
> *We sat in a room full of people*
> *and exchanged Christmas gifts.*
> *I received a lovely book.*
> *You, a dragonfly necklace.*
> *I thought it was a nice fit...*

Now, when I sit by a lonesome lake
and get lost in my mind's eye,
on my body gently lands
another dragonfly.

Your presence has never left me; it's with them,

creatures of joy, love, and transformation.
I'm never alone here.
I'm a part of this divine communication.

You gave me a gift;
It means more than you realize.
An unconditional love,
I've seen in your cosmic eyes.

DELIRIUM

In a delirium of night lights,
we're gazing into each other's eyes
longer than we should.
You're filling the space in my mind;
Falling's never felt so good.

Every caress is moving me
from one point to another:
through stars and the Milky Way.

Your lips are craving mine.
High frequencies are in the air
with the feelings you're trying to hide,
but my instincts whisper that you care.

I smell a sweet fragrance on your neck:
a mix of mandarin, jasmine, and vanilla flowers.
Even if I try to run, it pulls me right back,
leading to dreams where I am your lover.

We're exchanging our energies
with the highest vibrations.
I'm drowning in you
with all my sensations.

In a delirium of lights,
my heart has melted in your sight,
and when anyone asks for it now,
there's nothing to give; I lost it that night.

FOR YOU

We were playing hide and seek
in the warehouse
of our feelings.
"You're crazy," you said with a smile,
and I thought: *I'm crazy about you.*

My soul wandered too far from yours,
to a different country.
But you found me
somewhere in an aisle
with New Era caps and clothes.

And yet, I'm still trying to find myself
in infinite equations of this love.

I've always been turning the ordinary
into something special,
like a magician in a fairytale,
and every time you gazed at me
was the time when I fell

for you.

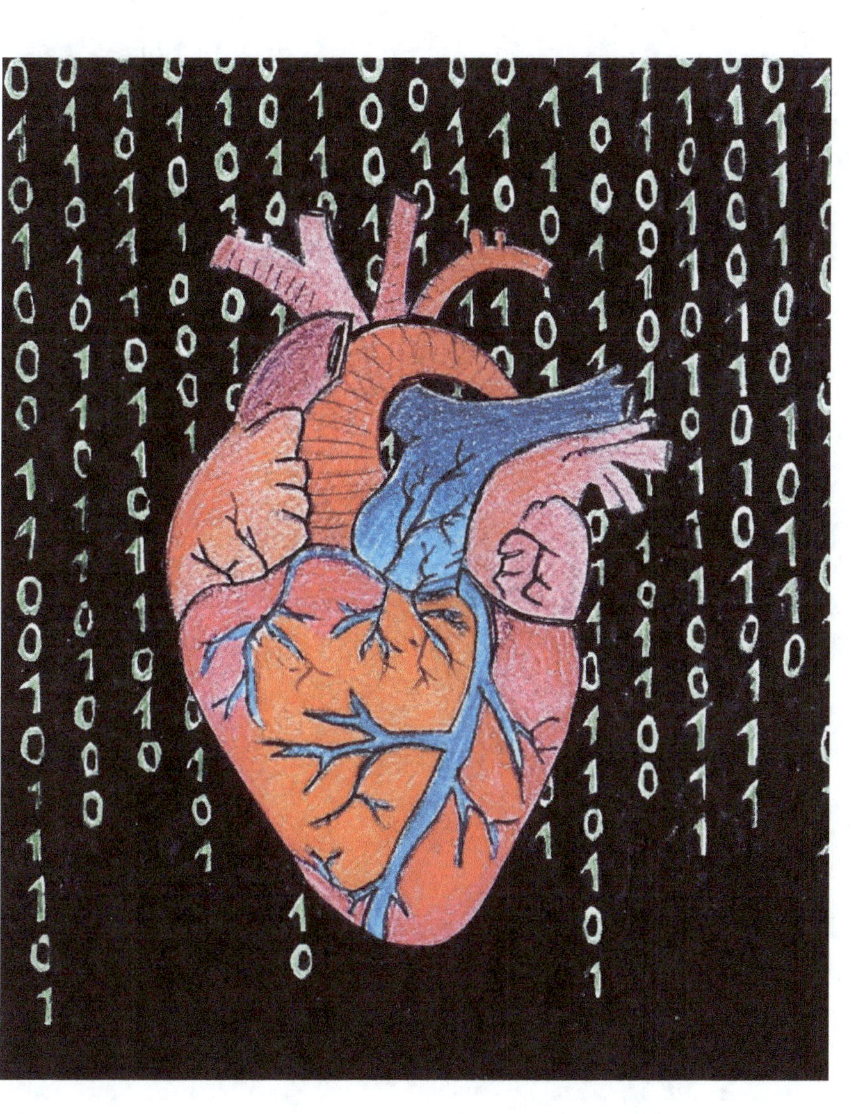

ABOUT THE AUTHOR

Lenka Dvorcakova was born in Presov, Slovakia. She attended art school from early childhood and was always interested in writing stories and poetry. She pursued Slovak, literature, and communication studies at the University of Presov, where she successfully graduated with a master's degree. A few years after graduation, she decided to leave her home country and start over in the Netherlands, where she was determined to write her debut book, *Crazy Game Called Life*. Lenka's life journey has been challenging but abundant. Spiritual awakening is never an easy path, but it brings a purpose to the people, opening their minds to all possibilities

www.ingramcontent.com/pod-product-compliance
Lightning Source LLC
Chambersburg PA
CBHW061257140726
47998CB00006B/2253